OVER TIME
PALO ALTO
1947–1980

OVER TIME
PALO ALTO
1947–1980

BEN HATFIELD WITH BARRY ANDERSON

Published by Arcadia Publishing
Charleston SC, Chicago IL, Portsmouth NH, San Francisco CA

Printed in the United States of America

Library of Congress Catalog Card Number: 2006931276

For all general information contact Arcadia Publishing at:
Telephone 843-853-2070
Fax 843-853-0044
E-mail sales@arcadiapublishing.com
For customer service and orders:
Toll-Free 1-888-313-2665

Visit us on the Internet at www.arcadiapublishing.com

To honor my father, Adrian R. Hatfield, a pioneer in aerial photography of the Bay Area from 1947 to 1979 and a communications and photojournalism major at Stanford University, class of 1938. His images documented changes in land use and growth over the last 50 years. The aerial photography business also led Hatfield into commercial real estate sales early in his career.

ADRIAN HATFIELD. Pictured here at Palo Alto Airport, Hatfield was one of the first aerial photographers in the Bay Area, establishing a business in Menlo Park in 1947. This book is a collection of his work.

CONTENTS

ACKNOWLEDGMENTS

I wish to thank Marge Hatfield, my loving mother and "Skydiving Mom," for supporting this endeavor and proofreading the manuscript. Also supportive were the Hatfield family and mentor and editor Chris Hogan. I thank Steve Staiger and Jack Parkhouse of the Palo Alto Historical Association, Dr. Andrew Cope of Stanford Children's Hospital, and Maggie Kimbal of the Green Library of Stanford University for their research assistance. I am grateful to Harry and Lisl Day, mentors and friends.

Additional thanks go to Alpine Beer Garden (my second office when not in the Palo Alto Library) and owner Molly Alexander and staff for staying open later than usual so Barry and I could organize the book. Author John Buck, who assisted with editing and support, and mentor Don McDonald both shared their love for history and for Palo Alto. Brad Anderson helped in writing captions. Thanks also for the moral support received from the California Writers Club in Sunnyvale.

Finally, I am grateful to the team of people at Arcadia Publishing who contributed their hard work and time to help complete this book: Hannah Clayborn, Christine Talbot, Scott Davis, and Devon Weston. Thanks also to brother-in-law Fred Harper, who worked for Hewlett-Packard over 20 years and helped with the accuracy of the electronics ERA and my other brother-in-law, Ed Oliver, who explained the development of Fairchild and later companies. And thanks to all my immediate family for their support. All images, unless otherwise noted, are courtesy of Adrian Hatfield and the author's personal collection.

INTRODUCTION

My father, Adrian Hatfield, attended Stanford University as a communications and photojournalism major and learned to love the area. When World War II began, he joined the Army Air Corps and was trained in Colorado Springs as an aerial photographer. He worked on the invasion plans of the European theater and was later sent to the Caribbean until the Japanese surrender on VJ Day.

My family came to Menlo Park, California, in 1947 and settled in a house near the Stanford Golf Course. There my father started Hatfield Aerial Surveys out of the garage, becoming one of the first aerial photographers in the Greater San Francisco Bay Area. He also worked in real estate in the late 1940s and early 1950s.

I used to go on many photographic missions with my father, usually flying out of Palo Alto Airport or San Carlos Airport (then called San Mateo County Airport). After we flew over Los Altos and reached Santa Clara and San Jose, we were really out in "the country." When the shoot was completed, he would let me use the smaller aerial camera. I took photographs of places with which I was familiar: the Stanford Tower and campus, Moffett Field, Palo Alto, and Menlo Park, or ocean shots along the coast of Half Moon Bay to Santa Cruz and Monterey. I displayed these photographs for a presentation in history class at school.

So many men like my father were coming home from the war, looking to buy homes and work in the area, which as a result experienced a building boom from 1949 through the 1960s. New homes sprang up all over the Santa Clara Valley. My father worked with realtors as well as large landowners and developers. He always had firsthand information about the new hot regions for expansion. I can remember all the housing tracts going up in Menlo Park and Palo Alto. South of that were orchards, farmland, and ranches.

My father always had his sights on Los Altos, and in 1960, he bought three acres of land by Neary Quarry and above Foothill Junior College, on Priscilla Lane. We built our new home in Los Altos Hills and had moved in by 1963. My father set up the new Hatfield Aerial Surveys shop in Los Altos Hills and during the next decade proceeded to capture on film the expansion of the Stanford Industrial Park, the birth of the Silicon Valley, and the expansion of the high-tech industry south from Palo Alto into Sunnyvale, Mountain View, and Santa Clara. My father also did work for the State of California, mapping the new 280 Freeway and 101 Freeway overpass changes and documenting the new junior colleges: Foothill Junior College, the College of San Mateo, Cañada Junior College, De Anza Junior College, and West Valley Junior College.

One of his most noted images was the 280-101-680 interchange in San Jose during the 1973 gasoline shortage. Many area residents remember the monster overpasses that ran nowhere and sat unfinished for four years during that time. The mayor of San Jose, Joe Colla, asked my father for some ideas to get funding to finish the eyesore. They came up with the scheme of placing an old Chevy on top of the ramp by crane in the wee hours of the morning. They waited until the next business day's peak traffic hour and lowered Joe Colla down by helicopter. Joe stretched out his arms with a gesture that said, "Where do I drive from here?" as my father shot away, capturing Joe's dilemma from different angles. Before the pair even got back to the airport, Gov. Jerry Brown had left a message for Colla telling him to get that damn car off the ramp now!

Nevertheless, the plan worked. The City of San Jose received funding four months later, and the project was successfully completed the subsequent year. The series of aerial photographs made headline news all over California and across the country. For over half a century, Hatfield Aerial Surveys has captured the changes in land use in the San Francisco Bay Area, the Santa Clara County region, and the East Bay from Oakland down to the Central Valley and south to Gilroy and Monterey.

My friend and caption collaborator Barry Anderson was born in 1947 in Palo Alto. Raised in nearby Menlo Park, he spent his entire early life exploring San Francisquito Creek, the old train stations, the trestle, and other area sights. After attending Fremont School, Hillview School, and Menlo-Atherton High School, he served in the army in the late 1960s. He also worked as an artist in San Francisco during the 1970s, creating T-shirt designs for the local rock music scene. Still living in Palo Alto, Anderson has an avid interest in American and local history. He has worked in the graphic arts field in one capacity or another all of his adult life.

From the preflight development of the first 10 years over Palo Alto, from 1930 to 1940, to the southward expansion and the Stanford Industrial Park and beyond, this book is an aerial glimpse into the city during its time of greatest transition. New builders flocked to the new area after World War II, and a building boom was on to house all the new residents. Citizens such as Eichler, Mackeller, Sterns and Price, and Barrett and Hilp became pioneers of the electronics boom. Palo Alto thus changed from ranch land to high tech in a very short time span.

This book is an invitation to view Palo Alto with my father and me, to see the changes in land use over the 35 postwar years, before Silicon Valley grew up around it. The seeds of Silicon Valley were truly Palo Alto and Stanford University; as Adrian Hatfield put it, the city produced everything "from apricot chips to silicon chips!"

By the late 1940s, Palo Alto had a population of 17,000, and the open land was nearly filled. Still they kept coming; by 1950, there was a population of 25,000, with new arrivals averaging three to five people a day. And that was only the beginning. Over the years, Palo Alto has emerged as a center for culture, education, high-tech electronics, science, and advanced medicine. This incredible community and its innovations continue to contribute greatly to the nation and the world today.

Author Ben Hatfield and caption collaborator Barry Anderson are pictured at Menlo Park Art and Antiques. The hot rod, a 1940 Ford panel delivery truck, was used on Hatfield Aerial Survey missions.

OPPOSITE: THE CIRCLE, 1948. Pictured here again is the Circle, Palo Alto's familiar traffic exchange, where University Avenue and Alma Street meet.

GATES TO THE CITY
1940–1960

Long before the Spanish explored the coastal areas of Half Moon Bay and ventured over the hills to the current location of Palo Alto, the Ohlone Indians lived in the region. The Twin Tall Trees was a meeting place of the native tribes who lived near San Francisquito Creek. The early Spanish explorers, led by Gaspar de Portola, came down from the Pacific Ocean to those same tall trees and marked them on their maps as *El Palo Alto*, or Tall Tree.

Later Mexican ranchers flocked to the area because of the open grazing land, the abundance of water, the rich, fertile soil, and the climate needed for cattle ranching and farming. Local rancho names included San Francisquito, Rinconada del Arroyo de San Francisquito, Rincon de San Francisquito, Pastoria de las Boregas, El Corte de Madero, and La Purisima Concepcion in what are now Los Altos Hills and Palo Alto. White settlers

displaced the owners of these ranchos in the mid-19th century.

Leland Stanford, one of the "Big Four" of the Central Pacific Railroad, and Timothy Hopkins, an early developer, lived in San Francisco. Stanford also owned a horse-trotting farm in the town of Mayfield, near what is now Stanford Hospital. While on vacation in Europe, Stanford's only son, Leland Jr., took ill and died soon thereafter. The Stanfords wanted to honor

their son by building a university in his name. While Stanford University was under construction, Stanford and Hopkins had a vision to create a town nearby the campus. Stanford signed a note for Hopkins, who purchased the land from Henry Seale and the Greer family and had it plotted into streets and lots. Hopkins initially named the community University Park, but Stanford preferred the old Spanish designation of Palo Alto.

Hopkins excavated land for roads, planted trees along the streets, and designated areas for parks. University Avenue was to be the heart of the new town. The first families arrived in 1890 and 1891, and the first homes were built on University, Emerson, and Webster Streets and Lytton Avenue. Commercial buildings sprang up in the downtown area on University Street, Lytton and Hamilton Avenues, and near the train station.

In many ways, Palo Alto and Stanford have always been connected. The first Palo Alto subdivision was College Terrace. In 1887, farmer and large landowner Alexander Gordon started subdividing his parcels, naming the streets after Eastern universities and colleges, with the intention of selling lots to Stanford professors and faculty. Gordon's development became part of Mayfield, which was incorporated in 1903 and later annexed into Palo Alto in 1925.

Early on, Palo Alto enjoyed many of the amenities of a larger city. Only 25 years after its spring 1894 incorporation, Palo Alto had its own utilities; water came first, then gas, then an electrical power plant, then sewers. All of these were city owned and operated in an age when most utility companies were private. Palo Alto had its own telephone system, bus system, major train station, airport, and active yacht harbor. Residents also enjoyed many theaters and parks. Later the Bayshore Freeway, also known as U.S. Highway 101, linked San Jose to San Francisco and brought many visitors to Palo Alto.

Natural waterways form some of the city's boundaries. Two of the creeks that run through Palo Alto, San Francisquito and Adobe, are also its riparian boundary lines. San Francisquito Creek flows down from Portola Valley and out to the bay and divides the town of Menlo Park from Palo Alto. Adobe Creek forms the boundary with Los Altos Hills. Matadero and Deer Creeks also run through Palo Alto.

By the start of the 20th century, Palo Alto's streets were laid out, though many of the area's giant white oaks were left in the center of these new roads. Soon automobiles began to run into the trees, and out-of-town drivers sued the city for damages. The city council proposed a plan to cut down all trees that grew more than one foot from the curb. The townspeople, even children, petitioned to "Save the Oaks." This movement symbolized the kind of town Palo Alto was becoming—intellectual and environmentally friendly. Citizens voted to save the beautiful oaks, and they painted the trunks of the trees white so motorists could more easily see them at night.

Palo Alto was also kindhearted. Starting in World War I and continuing through the Great Depression and World War II, Palo Altans donated money for The Shelter, a local organization that fed and housed unemployed men. The unemployed could "earn a supper" and a warm place to sleep for a period of up to 48 hours.

Since education of the young was a priority in town, good morals and behavior also became important. The Stanford faculty approved an ordinance banning the sale of tobacco within 1,000 feet of a school. Early on, founder Leland Stanford made provisions in a letter written to Timothy Hopkins that no alcoholic beverages were to be sold or stored within a two-mile radius of Stanford's campus. This letter became a restriction written into the deeds of land sold to businesses in Palo Alto, and it was strictly enforced with a fine of up to $300—a great deal of money in those days. Then in 1909, the Prohibition Nomination Party changed the two-mile law to just one and a half miles around the campus. This law remained in place until 1970, when the superior court ruled that the university could not prevent owners of Henry's restaurant in the President Hotel from serving alcoholic beverages. The first were served legally at the restaurant in May 1971.

Throughout this era, numerous saloons operated in Menlo Park and Mayfield, and an area known as Whiskey Gulch developed just over the two-mile limit in East Palo Alto. No doubt many students found their way to these areas over the years.

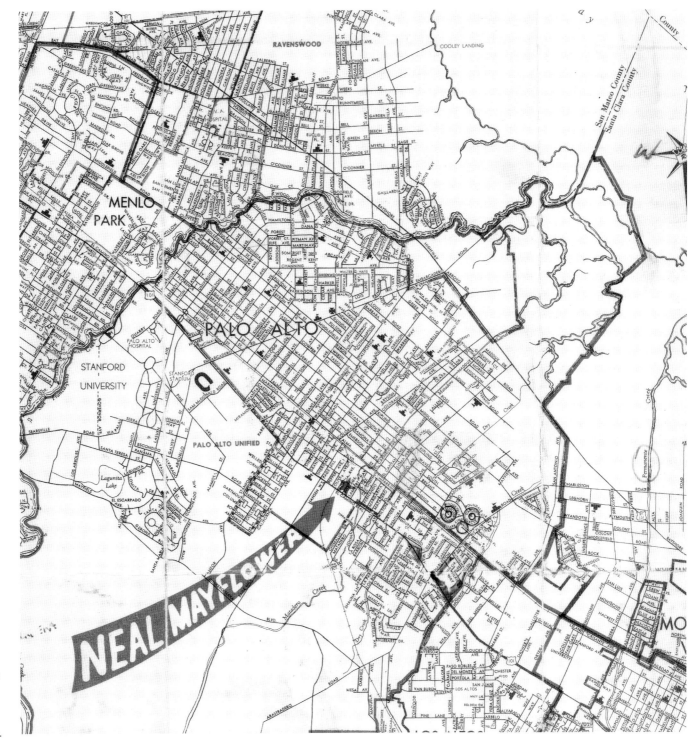

MAP, 1947. The moving van and storage company, Neal Mayflower, developed this map, depicting Palo Alto, Menlo Park, South Palo Alto, and a portion of Los Altos to the south. Businesses that made their money from construction, moving, and the like were benefited by the postwar influx of new homes and families to Palo Alto.

DAVENPORT PREFIX, 1947. In the above view, note the Christmas tree in the middle of University Avenue near the underpass and the decorations stretched out across the street. The building on the corner of University and High Street is the old Fraternal Hall, built in 1898. It now hosts a popular sushi restaurant on the first floor. In the lower left corner, at Lytton and Alma, is the Greyhound bus depot. Inside was a comfortable waiting room, complete with a sit-down coffee shop. Palo Alto's first telephone company operated out of the building with the pitched roof at upper center. At right is a *c.* 1947 advertisement for the Pacific Telephone and Telegraph Company. Some of the prefixes in the region at this time were Davenport (DA) in Palo Alto, Emerson (EM) in Redwood City, and Lytell (LY) in Mountain View.

How to deal with the Dial...
for best telephone service

After lifting the receiver, always listen for dial tone (a steady humming sound) to make sure the equipment is ready to receive your call.

If your finger slips or you make any other mistake while dialing, replace the receiver and wait a few seconds. Then start the call over again.

Learn to identify the sound signals that tell how your call is progressing: Ringing Signal—a "burring" tone repeated at regular intervals, indicates the telephone called is ringing. Busy Signal—a steady "buzz-buzz-buzz" sound, indicates the line called is in use. Dial Again Signal—a continuous hum alternately rising and falling in pitch indicates some mistake has occurred on the call.

Remember that your dial telephone is made of precision parts. Rough, careless treatment may cause it to function poorly and impede the good service it gives when properly used.

The Pacific Telephone and Telegraph Company

GEORGE PADDLEFORD'S CADILLAC AGENCY. The advertisement at left, appearing in the February 1950 *Palo Alto Times*, promotes Paddleford's automobile dealership, located on the corner of Emerson Street and Homer Avenue. Below is a *c.* 1947 image of the business. The George S. Paddleford building has since been enlarged and is now home to Whole Foods Market. The small structure in the upper left is a Mexican restaurant. All the buildings in the foreground remain today.

WAVERLY AND HOMER STREETS, 1947. St. Thomas Aquinas Church occupies the corner in this view. A scene in the 1970s movie *Harold and Maude* was filmed in this church. The houses at upper right have been replaced by a park, and the home at lower right with the long driveway and the white square in the backyard is now the Museum of American Heritage.

MAILMAN ON HIS MORNING ROUTE, 1947. This photograph was taken for an article in *See and Play* magazine written by Hazel Glaister Robertson, founder of the Palo Alto Children's Theatre. (Courtesy Palo Alto Children's Theatre Archive, photograph by Anita Fowler.)

ALMA AND HAMILTON STREETS, 1947. At this time, the area was known as Auto Row. If one wanted a car in the 1940s or 1950s, he traveled to Alma Street, south of University Avenue. The Circle appears on the left. In the upper right, the two little houses with white peaked roofs are still there, as are many of these buildings. The dog kennel in the foreground is now gone.

PHONE DIRECTORY ADVERTISEMENTS, 1947. Shown above are advertisements for Hagen and Bell Auto Sales, at 217 Alma Street in Palo Alto. Above left is an ad for Bill Young's Service, at 849 High Street. The latter remains in operation today. To the right are announcements promoting G. A. Baer Studebaker and Hagen and Bell Lincoln Mercury. Over time, the dealerships on the one-time Auto Row began to move closer to El Camino Real. Note the Davenport prefix in all the advertisements.

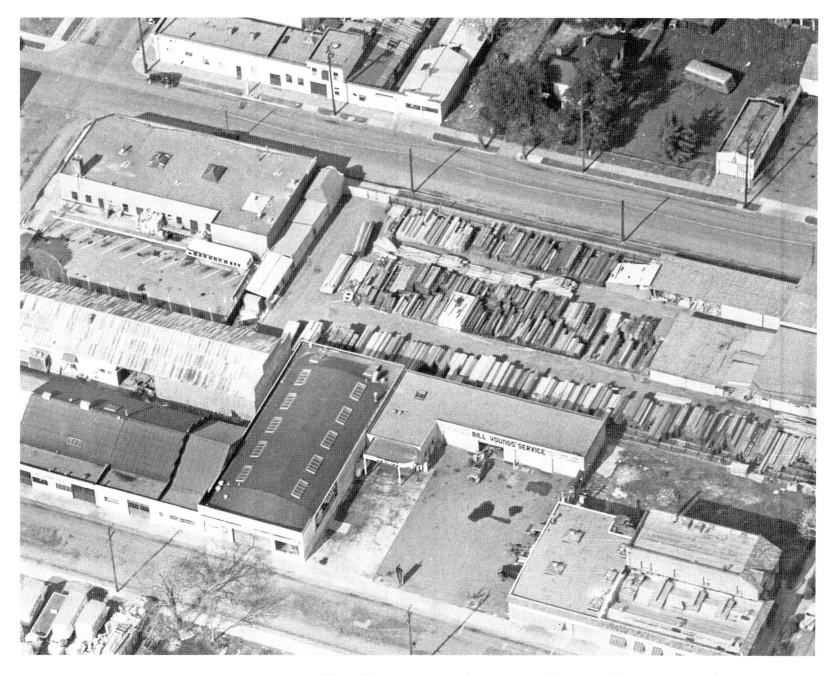

HIGH STREET BETWEEN HOMER AND CHANNING STREETS, 1947. Alma Street was the place to buy or repair a car. These four square blocks west of Alma contained Bill Young's Service (pictured at center) and George Paddleford's Cadillac dealership, whose advertisements appear on the previous page. The convenience of being able to shop multiple dealerships within a small geographic area is a trend that has persisted to today.

ALMA STREET NEAR UNIVERSITY AVENUE, 1947. The Don Hampton Dodge Plymouth dealership is pictured here. The presence of the adjacent Packard dealership further verifies the date of this image, as the Packard Motor Car Company went out of business in 1958.

CHANNING AVENUE AND ALMA STREET, 1947. The Kaiser-Frazer automobile dealership was housed in a building now occupied by Palo Alto Ace Hardware.

NOW—Or in the FUTURE

LET US KEEP YOUR CAR IN SHAPE
BODY & FENDER REPAIRS—
Complete Wreck Work **WELDING · PAINTING**
RADIATORS— *Recored · Repaired · Cleaned*
"JOHN M. MOE"
MENLO BODY FENDER & RADIATOR WORKS
633 Live Oak Ave., Menlo Park
Call **PALO ALTO 2-4255**

RADIATORS

RADIATORS REBUILT
CLEANED · REPAIRED
WE RECORE ALL MAKES

Guaranteed
Not to Overheat

EFFICIENT SERVICE

AUTO REPAIR

ELLISON'S

AUTO BODY · FENDER
& RADIATOR WORKS

18 Years in Business in Palo Alto

841 ALMA

Phone **PALO ALTO 4822**

AUTO REPAIR ADVERTISEMENTS, 1947. Here Menlo Body Fender and Radiator Works uses futuristic cars to advertise its capability in repairing the peninsula's automobiles "Now—Or in the future." Ellison's Auto Body Fender and Radiator Works, still at the same location, guarantees that radiators rebuilt by its mechanics will not overheat.

ALMA AND HOMER STREETS, 1947. The gas station on the corner now hosts a BMW repair shop, and the building across the street operates as Ole's Car Shop. To the right is Channing Avenue, where the corner building has become Palo Alto Ace Hardware. At one time, this entire block comprised the Peninsula Creamery bottling plant. The trucks grouped together in the center are Peninsula Creamery trucks, used to transport milk from the dairy at the Stanford barn to the bottling plant. The structures in the foreground bear signs reading "Horabin Hay" and "Horabin Bros. Ready to mix concrete." The area is now the site of Palo Alto Medical Center. The building with the nonparallel sides near the train tracks was used as a concert hall for a brief time in the 1970s. Jerry Garcia and the Grateful Dead played music at Homer's Warehouse many times.

This certificate entitles you to one Free Milkshake at Peninsula Creamery

We like to think of "The Penn" as a Stanford tradition—one of long standing.

For years Peninsula Creamery's "famous shake" has been popular among students on The Farm. As a Stanford freshman you have a special invitation to visit Peninsula Creamery. Come in and meet our famous "Mr. Milkshake."

Peninsula Creamery

HAMILTON AT EMERSON   DAvenport 3-3176

PENINSULA CREAMERY. This restaurant was a favorite hangout for Palo Alto High School and Stanford students. Renowned for its milk shakes and burgers, Peninsula Creamery remains very popular with locals. In these 1940s advertisements, note the prices listed: a milk shake for 15¢, a malted milk for 20¢, and a steak sandwich for 20¢.

BAYSHORE HIGHWAY AND UNIVERSITY AVENUE, EAST PALO ALTO, 1947. In this northward view, the building with the tall spire is Auten's Restaurant. A motel is located in the lower right corner.

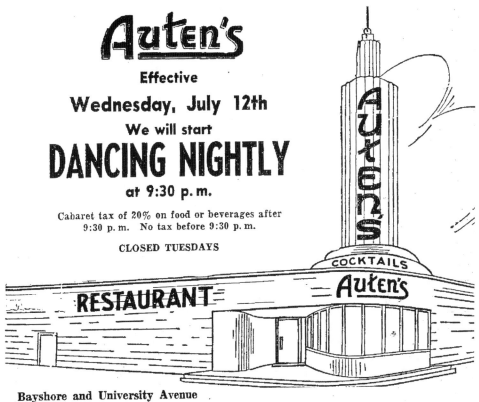

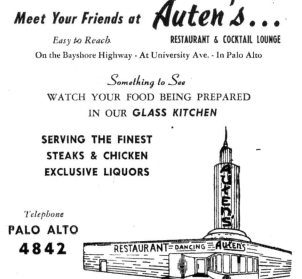

AUTEN'S RESTAURANT. This restaurant was a favorite of Palo Alto residents during the 1940s and 1950s. Note the same spire pictured in these advertisements as is visible in the aerial view on the previous page. The Women's Army Air Corps (WAC) uses this page to promote its motto of "Hope as Well as Help." Many Bay Area WACs learned how to fly at the Palo Alto Airport, after which their duties involved ferrying fighter and bomber aircrafts to the front lines in England.

University Avenue as It Meets Bayshore Highway, 1947. Bayshore Highway (101) appears above, while Crescent Street occupies the lower portion of this view. The downtown area in the center was commonly called Whiskey Gulch because it lay just outside the no-alcohol boundary imposed by Stanford University on its immediately surrounding businesses. Despite the nickname, it was a nice little community with grocery stores, diners, and retail outlets. The area is now the site of a major office complex and a five-star hotel. The IKEA building stands on the other side of 101.

Palo Alto Police Officer, 1947. This photograph, also taken for *See and Play* magazine, features a local police officer on his beat. It is possible that this officer worked to enforce the boundaries of Stanford's alcohol ban while patrolling in Whiskey Gulch—at least up until 1971, when the ban was finally lifted. (Courtesy Palo Alto Children's Theatre Archive, photograph by Anita Fowler.)

University Avenue and Bayshore Highway, 1947. This view looks toward downtown Palo Alto. Whiskey Gulch, University Avenue, and Crescent Street are at upper center. Also worth noting is the prevalence of gas stations—of course, to accommodate the many families who drove and even purchased their cars in Palo Alto.

CONGRATULATIONS TO THE CLASS OF '54

Del Boccignone and Kay Blackmore keep score for Steve Brown while Barbara McCall and Pete Dowell wait their turn.

INDIAN BOWL
735 EMERSON STREET

Pete Bonnet and Mary Swift find that Crow Pharmacy has a wide variety of things that make shaving easy . . . for gift and for use.

CROW PHARMACY
PRESCRIPTION SPECIALISTS
547 BRYANT ST.
DAVENPORT 3-4169
PALO ALTO, CALIFORNIA

MODELED BY DIANA TUCKER AND NILES ELWOOD

Grande's Shoes
CAMPUS STYLES for STUDENTS

ROBLEE, PEDWINS — COVER GIRLS, TEEN AGERS

MODELED BY BRICK ARMSTRONG AND MARY JO FITERRE

Hofman JEWELER

Suzi Linn holds a handsome leather case as Chris Ey points out the popular "VIKING" binder at C & C.

Congdon & Crome
STATIONERY
OFFICE SUPPLIES
PALO ALTO, CALIFORNIA

Jean Wentworth, Sally Gill, and Margo Boothe model the smartest in spring cottons at The Colony.

the colony
TOWN and COUNTRY CLOTHES

PALO ALTO • CALIFORNIA

PALO ALTO HIGH SCHOOL YEARBOOK ADVERTISEMENTS, 1950s. Featured in the *Madrono* yearbook are promotions for Grande's Shoes, Hofman Jeweler, and Congdon and Crome Stationery, among many others. All of the models are actual Palo Alto High School students.

UNIVERSITY AVENUE, 1948. This view shows the intersections of Emerson, Ramona, and Bryant Streets. The Stanford Theater building remains, as does the old police court and firehouse in the upper right corner, though the structure is now a senior center. Other businesses include Dr. Horowitz, D.D.S; Stanford Bowl; Congdon and Crome; Rexall Drugs; Hofman Jeweler; Ruperts; and Hinks department store. The future site of Lytton Plaza is at the left corner. Nola's Restaurant and Bar currently occupies a spot at lower center. The alley at lower right held the entrance to the old 42nd Street Restaurant.

FIREMAN IN HIS TRUCK, 1947. This truck may very well have been stationed at the firehouse pictured in the upper right corner of the above image. (Courtesy Palo Alto Children's Theatre Archive, photograph by Anita Fowler.)

THE VARSITY THEATRE. A February 1950 *Palo Alto Times* advertisement (left) promotes the Varsity Theatre, located on University Avenue. The movie playing is *Battleground*, released in 1949. In later years, the venue changed into a music hall, playhouse, and restaurant. *The Rocky Horror Picture Show* was a Saturday night tradition for a couple years. The building now hosts Borders Books. Several automobiles are parked in front of the theater in the 1948 image (below), as a trip out to the movies in those days was still somewhat of a special event. The buildings to the left and right are still there. One of them was the early location of St. Michaels Ally, a beatnik hangout where early folksingers played music while people enjoyed coffee. (Left, courtesy Palo Alto Library.)

WAVERLY STREET AND HAMILTON AVENUE, 1948. Note the Varsity Theatre at the upper center of this image. Purity Market (left) featured a form of architecture common in the postwar landscape—a Quonset hut, a prefabricated structure developed in the war by the navy and later sold to the public. In stark contrast to the domed corrugated steel is the Victorian tower facing the hut on Waverly Street. The large apartment house at upper right is now the site of the Garden Court Hotel and one of the famous Il Fornaio Restaurants.

EMERSON STREET AND FOREST AVENUE, 1948. Forest Avenue and Emerson Street are shown in the upper portion of this view. One can see the old Indian Bowl logo in the concrete sidewalk near the upper right corner; it is the white spot in the doorway of the large flat-roofed building. That structure is now gone, but that beautiful old logo remains in the sidewalk.

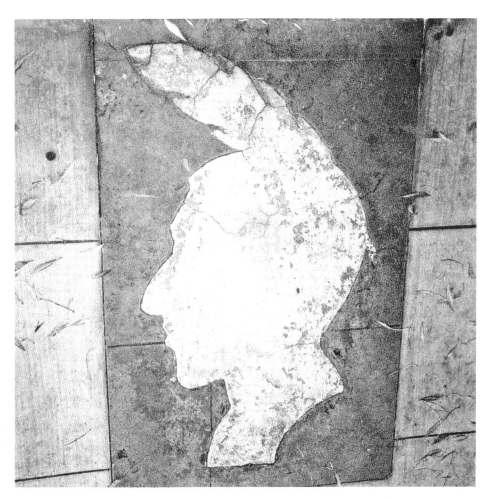

INDIAN BOWL. This concrete emblem, seen above right and from a great distance on the previous page, is all that is left of Indian Bowl. The bowling alley chose its name to appear affiliated with Stanford's Native American athletic theme. The emblem, still stamped in the sidewalk on Emerson between Homer and Forest Streets, was situated just outside the doorway, and one would pass over it when entering the small downtown bowling alley. Below is a 1940s advertisement for the popular hangout spot.

THE INDIAN BOWL

- Open daily 11 to 1 a.m.
- Leagues play M. W. F., 7 to 11 p.m.; Th. 7 to 9 p.m.
- No leagues Fri., Sat., or Sun.
- Fountain service daily 11 to 1 a.m.

735 Emerson St.   DAvenport 2-3411

AUTO DEALERSHIPS, 1948. The Studebaker dealership occupied this corner along with Don L. Morris. Both buildings remain today. Note the back of the Weltner Pontiac used car dealership on High Street.

MAGAZINE ADVERTISEMENT, 1947. G. A. Baer Studebaker Sales and Service was situated at the corner of Forest Avenue and Alma Street in Palo Alto. This advertisement ran in the *Palo Alto Times* in February 1950.

32

DOWNTOWN PALO ALTO, LOOKING EAST, 1948. San Francisquito Creek dips into the image at the top. The Luck Market sign rises above the Lytton and Ramona intersection (upper center, large white square). The President and Cardinal were the main downtown hotels of this era. University Avenue and Alma Street appear at lower left. The lower portion of this view now hosts two major hotels.

OVERVIEW OF DOWNTOWN PALO ALTO, 1948. This view looks north to the boundary line between Palo Alto and Menlo Park: San Francisquito Creek.

DOWNTOWN PALO ALTO, 1949. Emerson Street intersects with Lytton Avenue at lower left, while the Circle occupies the lower right. The Downing Block building stands on Hamilton and Emerson across from the Peninsula Grill, one of the oldest surviving coffee shops in town. It used to be the original Peninsula Creamery. The two high-rise apartment buildings at upper left are the Casa Real buildings and the Laning Chateau, built in 1927. At left center is the Hamilton Building, which houses the university art store. As seen here, a gas station was on nearly every corner in those days, just as now.

MILK DELIVERY, 1947. When residents did not have time to stop in at the Peninsula Creamery or one of the many coffee shops in downtown for their cup of coffee with cream, milk delivery people, like the one pictured here, home delivered dairy products that came straight from the source. Piers Dairy was the largest dairy provider on the peninsula at this time and would have contributed products to both private and commercial consumers. (Courtesy Palo Alto Children's Theatre Archive, photograph by Anita Fowler.)

PALO ALTO, LOOKING TOWARD MENLO PARK, 1956. Taken from above Embarcadero Road at El Camino, this panoramic view looks northwest. El Camino runs diagonally toward the upper right corner, and Highway 101 is to the right next to the bay. In the left distance, at the upper edge of the photograph, are Crystal Springs Reservoir and Half Moon Bay. Crystal Springs is a water-storage facility that is part of San Francisco's famed Hetch Hetchy water system, which originates inside of Yosemite National Park.

WHISKEY GULCH, 1957. Once located at Highway 101 and University Avenue, here Whiskey Gulch experiences new roadway construction at its center. Until 1971, all of the stores and restaurants within a two-mile radius of Stanford University were prohibited from selling liquor, so the area was deemed "Whiskey Gulch" to denote the dry section. Also visible is the Reno Club, serving "Just Good Grub," in the narrow building near the highway. The Reno Club had real silver dollars set in the top of its wooden bar.

Dinah's Shack

<u>Dares</u> to introduce fine dinners
at $1.95 complete, including dessert

DINAH'S SHACK. This *c.* 1949 advertisement reads, "<u>Dares</u> to introduce fine dinners at $1.95 complete, including dessert." The restaurant was associated with a motor-home park and swimming pool.

37

DOWNTOWN PALO ALTO, 1975. In this view toward Stanford University, Stanford Shopping Center is seen to the right, while Page Mill Road curves its way out to Highway 280 in the left distance. This image provides a glimpse of what is to come for Palo Alto. The tall building in the lower left became the first skyscraper along University Avenue. Where University intersects El Camino Real, in the distance, the road bends and becomes Palm Drive, the main thoroughfare into Stanford University. Note the famously wooded grounds of the college.

OPPOSITE: MAYFIELD SCHOOL, 1947. This early elementary school, built in 1923 and razed in the 1980s, was located in the town of Mayfield before annexation by Palo Alto. Dairy cows graze in the distance, while El Camino Real appears in the foreground.

CIVIC BUILDINGS AND COMMUNITY LIFE

From the beginning, Palo Alto was successful because it was run and developed with the help of Stanford professors who donated their time on the planning committees and on the city council. Stanford professors, who often held law degrees and still taught classes at the university, acted as mayors, city engineers, and city managers. These Stanford faculty members, mostly from the fields of science, engineering, and law, were the city fathers. They will be referred to as such, or as the Palo Alto planning team, throughout this chapter.

Palo Alto was spunky. Early on, it established and retained ownership of its major utilities. It owned the city electrical plant on Embarcadero Road, the water and gas utilities, and its own sewage treatment plant.

In 1912, a private Redwood City company was supplying power to a processing plant in East Palo Alto. The company failed to ask Palo Alto for permission to install power poles and lines throughout the city. The firm installed them on a holiday, thinking that it could get away with the scheme and later persuade Palo Alto to purchase its power. Palo Alto, however, was set in its ways, and when the city fathers found out about the poles, they got together a crew to remove them completely. The aggressive power company's name happened to be Pacific Gas and Electric (PG&E)! Palo Alto later told PG&E where their poles and wires could be reclaimed, of course, after repayment for the cost of removal.

Water came from the Hetch Hetchy Dam, owned by the City and County of San Francisco. In 1934, a sewage treatment plant was installed out to the San Francisco Bay. In the 1950s and 1960s, secondary plants were built to separate out the silver and

copper compounds created by the new high-tech electronic companies in the area. Palo Alto incinerated its refuse, and the result helped to fill in parts of the bay. The city later used the Cooley Landing dump site in San Mateo County.

Palo Alto has used every mode of transportation from horse and buggy to trains, trolley cars, bicycles, and on to the automobile. Logging roads brought timber down out of Woodside and Redwood City to the lumber mills. Searsville (now Sand Hill) and Arastradero Roads were widely used for timber hauling. El Camino Real, meaning "the King's Highway," and Middle Road (later Middlefield Road) were traveled by all.

Traffic jams started early, as soon as the automobile became widely employed. These jams were created by the Southern Pacific Railway train, which stopped in town daily to pick up commuters going to San Francisco. The train had so many passengers each morning and evening that automobile traffic came to a standstill for long periods of time. This prevented shoppers from getting in and out of town. The city fathers came up with a solution: an underpass at Palm and University Avenues, beneath the train station. The new underpass, begun in 1938 and completed in 1941, eliminated much of the congestion. To further reduce congestion, Highway 101 was later constructed, linking San Jose with San Francisco. It quickly earned the nickname "Bloody Bayshore" because of the many head-on collisions that occurred before the addition of median barriers.

Later a very controversial measure was passed: the widening of Oregon Avenue for the new Oregon Expressway. This act razed many homes, forcing residents to relocate to Palo Alto or leave the area completely. But the Oregon Expressway did alleviate the traffic jams caused by people going to and from work in the new industrial complex. Another major widening project was San Antonio Road at the 101 freeway.

Then, of course, came air travel. In 1929, Stanford Flying Field was going full force at Stanford Avenue and El Camino Real until area residents complained about noise and air traffic. In 1933, the airfield was moved to become part of Palo Alto Airport near Highway 101 (Bayshore), adjacent to the bay. Many World War II pilots were trained to fly at Palo Alto Airport and then at Eagle Field in Fresno. Eagle Field sponsors yearly reunions of its wartime pilots and mechanics, who dress in their uniforms. Nurses and doctors all dress in officer's attire and dance to music from the 1940s, like Glen Miller. When I attend, I really enjoy meeting these old Fly Boys. Palo Alto Airport was top rated in 1947, and in 1967, a tower was built.

Rinconada Park, where city hall was located from 1952 to 1970, is now a cultural center with art classes, workshops, concerts, and a round swimming pool. Rinconada Pool, seen in many of the following photographs, was originally used as a cooling station for the Palo Alto city power plant. Mitchell Park on East Meadow was named after J. Pearce Mitchell, a Palo Alto councilman, Stanford professor, and later mayor. Hoover Pavilion, still used today, was *the* hospital until the Stanford Medical Hospital was completed in 1959. In 1991, Lucile Salter Packard Children's Hospital was opened in the same area.

Education maintained a primary interest in Palo Alto. Leland Stanford wanted schools and education to be Palo Alto's main business, serving everyone from kindergartners to graduate students. Many people had come to Palo Alto just for the school system, and the city took great measures to offer college preparatory programs, which often led to that great moment of graduating from Stanford. The growing technology industry, spurred on by Stanford faculty and graduates, also supported education. David Packard and William Hewlett, founders of the now-global technology company bearing their names, served on the board of education of the Palo Alto Unified School District. The board determined that each district in Palo Alto should build one to three new schools per year.

Dr. Henry Gunn, school superintendent from 1950 to 1961, saw an immediate need for higher math and new science technology in the education curriculum. This training in computer sciences and "new math" led California to the highest levels in advanced placement tests, unsurpassed anywhere. H. M. Gunn High School was completed on Arastradero Road in 1964 and named in honor of Dr. Gunn.

The board of education had plans for a junior college as far back as 1920. In 1957, board members realized their dream when they got financing from bond issues to build the new Foothill Junior College (now referred to as Foothill Community College) in Los Altos Hills. In the same Community College District, De Anza Junior College was finished in 1967. Palo Alto thus offered a complete educational system.

MAYFIELD ELEMENTARY SCHOOL, 1947. The above image shows downtown South Palo Alto. Contributor Barry Anderson's family resided in College Terrace in the late 1930s and early 1940s. Hundreds of schoolchildren living in the area wore the incredible maze of footpaths through the fields surrounding the school, visible here. The peculiarly shaped building on El Camino Real at center has been a restaurant since the 1940s. It is now the Olive Garden. In the past, it operated variously as the Chick Drive-In, the Bonanders Drive-In, and the Shirt-Tail Restaurant. Below left, the school is surrounded by open land and orchards. Page Mill Road and El Camino are visible in the upper right, near the long building; a dairy farm occupies the lower left corner.

THE START OF THE STANFORD INDUSTRIAL PARK. In 1947, after the invention of the transistor at Bell Laboratories in New Jersey, Stanford University professors and faculty had the foresight to set aside land where companies in the burgeoning electronics industry could establish themselves and expand. The Stanford Industrial Park was created, with the first tenant, Varian (far left), arriving in 1952. Other businesses to move in the 1950s were Hewlett-Packard in 1955 and Lockheed Missiles and Space that same year. At the center of the image, Mayfield Elementary School is again visible.

BARRON PARK SCHOOL, 1948. This school was built next to Matadero Creek. Lamata Way is at the left, and Josina Street is at the right.

BOARD OF EDUCATION

Mrs. M. Ruth Stone, Mrs. Pearl S. Shreve, Mr. C. W. Lockwood, Mr. Francis E. Whitmer, Mrs. Ruth Crary, Dr. John Almack

The governing body of the Palo Alto School District, with control over the high school as well as all other Palo Alto schools, is the Board of Education. The Board is composed of five members elected by the voters of Palo Alto, one new member being elected each year. The board has charge of all policy-making with regard to the schools, and of raising and expending tax money for the support of the schools. A superintendent, appointed by the Board, acts as executive head of the school system, and the Board works in cooperation with him.

Officers of the Board of Education are Mr. Francis E. Whitmer, Mrs. Pearl S. Shreve, Dr. John C. Almack, Mrs. Ruth C. Crary, and Mrs. M. Ruth Stone. Mr. Charles W. Lockwood served his first year as Superintendent of the Palo Alto Schools this year and acted as secretary to the Board.

PALO ALTO BOARD OF EDUCATION. The 1942 Palo Alto High School yearbook featured a small visual biography of that year's board of education. Charged with overseeing the high school as well as other Palo Alto schools, the board was composed of five members and the city superintendent. Pictured here from left to right are M. Ruth Stone, Pearl S. Shreve, C. W. Lockwood (Palo Alto Schools superintendent), Francis E. Whitmer, Ruth Crary, and Dr. John Almack.

PALO ALTO HIGH SCHOOL, 1947. The airplanes in the lower part of the image are old World War II surplus used for teaching aviation and engine repair. The upper portion is the future site of the Town and Country Village shopping center. El Camino Real and Embarcadero are at upper left, while the railroad tracks and Alma Street are to the right. In the center, one can see the old Greer House, which was torn down in 1953 to make way for the shopping center.

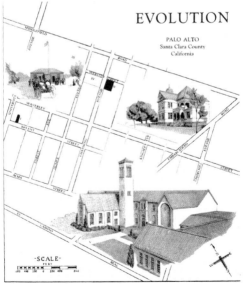

EVOLUTION

PALO ALTO
Santa Clara County
California

THE EVOLUTION OF PALO ALTO HIGH SCHOOL. Above is an image of the high school in 1949, also from the *Madrono*. Pictured at left is a map and timeline of Palo Alto's public schools from 1894 to 1918, taken from the 1947 *Madrono* yearbook.

-SCALE-
FEET

I. First public school — where Telephone Co. is at present. As pictured, the building was a small, wooden frame with a flag pole. It was erected by the carpenters in town in 1894.

II. The first high school classes were held in the second story of this grammar school building, which stood where the Channing soccer field is now.

III. This is the location of the first separate high school building. It was donated by Mrs. Zschokke in 1897 for use as a high school until the city could build one of its own. It is still standing as a remodelled home in its original location of 526 Forest. For a picture, see page nine.

IV. Channing school was the first city high school. It was erected in 1901 for a cost of twenty thousand five hundred dollars.

V. Our own Palo Alto Senior High School was built in 1918.

PALO ALTO HIGH SCHOOL ACTIVITIES. Color guard in the lead, the high school band (above) marches down University Avenue in the early 1940s. The jerseys on the varsity track team members (left) feature Viking wings on a *P*, representing Palo Alto and the school's Viking mascot. (Courtesy Palo Alto High School yearbook.)

VARSITY TRACK

1. VARSITY: Back row: Coach Ray, Munby, Tarp, Simons, Knaus, Stratton, Kizer, Working, Bishop
Front row: Ahumada, Mueller, Barnes, Cowdery, Rael, Mayock.
2. LIGHTWEIGHTS: Wood, Davis, Redeker, Jackson, Reynolds, Nichols, Anderson, Miller, Coach Ray.
3. Working, Rael, Barnes
4. Stratton and Cowdery
5. Practice jump

50

Palo Alto High School Grounds, 1947. This school still operates at the same location on Embarcadero Road and El Camino Real. Many of the buildings have been replaced.

GUNN HIGH SCHOOL, ARASTRADERO AND MIRANDA STREET, 1967. The area at lower right is a fruit orchard with a farmhouse and a water tower, part of the lands of Alta Mesa Memorial Park.

SYNTEX GROUNDS, 1979. Shown in this photograph are the biotechnology pioneer Syntex and the Veterans Hospital.

HOOVER TOWER, 1947. Lightning struck this great Stanford landmark's sandstone finial during the 1970s and blew it to bits. It has since been replaced.

STANFORD'S MEMORIAL COURT AND MAIN QUAD, C. 1947. In the above image, note the open space and abundance of parking, unlike the gridlock of today. Memorial Hall is located in the lower portion of the photograph, across from Hoover Tower. The area between the two now includes a large fountain. In the image below, at the upper right behind the chapel is a small, dark wooden tower. This tower held the bells taken from the Memorial Chapel when it collapsed in the 1906 earthquake. The bells stayed there until they were moved to a nearby location in the 1970s. In the early days, the loop in the foreground was a pond filled with fish and waterfowl.

THE GREAT STANFORD STADIUM, 1948. Built in 1921, this stadium held about 85,500 fans. Some of the athletes who coached or played here include Ernie Nevers, Glenn "Pop" Warner, Frankie Albert, John Ralston, Heisman Trophy winner Jim Plunkett, Chuck Taylor, John Brodie, Bill Walsh, John Elway, and Gene Washington, to name a few. Stanford Stadium was home to Stanford football teams nicknamed "the VOW Boys" in the 1930s, "the WOW Boys" in the 1940s, and the Thunder Chickens of the 1960s and 1970s. The San Francisco 49ers played the Miami Dolphins here in Super Bowl XIX. Stanford Stadium was demolished in 2005 and rebuilt.

DRY LAKE LAGUNITA, 1948. In this view looking east, Dry Lake Lagunita is pictured in the lower right corner. The open land around the campus was owned by Leland Stanford. Sand Hill Road did not run all the way to El Camino Real in 1948. Sand Hill Road was formerly called Searsville Road in the late 1800s and early 1900s. Highway 280 would later be built in the distant rolling hills.

STANFORD MEDICAL CENTER UNDER CONSTRUCTION, C. 1957. Sand Hill Road and San Francisquito Creek run across the top of the above left photograph. The old Stanford anatomy building is visible at the bottom. Above right, note the line of eucalyptus trees running along Governors Lane. Leland Stanford's house, now gone, stood at the end of this lane at lower left.

STANFORD MEDICAL CENTER, COMPLETED. Medical center construction was finished in 1959. The above left view, depicting Governors Lane, looks northeast over Stanford Hospital and Stanford Shopping Center to Middlefield Road in Menlo Park. Above right, a close-up image from 1962 shows an abundance of empty lots. In the distance is the chemistry building, along with the Stanford campus loop.

PALO ALTO HOSPITAL, 1947. Built in 1931 and reopened in 1965 as Hoover Pavilion, the early Stanford Hospital is pictured here in 1947. The open land surrounding the building would eventually be developed into Stanford Shopping Center in 1955. Palm Drive and El Camino are in the upper portion of the image on the left. A large, square fishpond was located behind the hospital. Also note the gates to the campus on Palm Drive. Barry Anderson was born at this hospital at just about the time these photographs were taken.

PALO ALTO VETERANS HOSPITAL UNDER CONSTRUCTION, 1955. Gunn High School and Syntex were just vacant fields at this time. Running along the bottom are Ilima Way and Laguna Avenue. The hospital is at the center of the image.

HILLVIEW AVENUE. The above left photograph, taken near the Veterans Affairs Hospital, shows the region around Hillview and Miranda Avenues in 1962. The road cutting off the upper right no longer exists. In the above right image, the Veterans Hospital is located at upper center, and the intersection of Hillview and Foothill Expressway can clearly be seen. The main hospital in this photograph has been torn down and rebuilt on the same site.

VIEW LOOKING NORTH TO PALO ALTO, C. 1964. This aerial view over Arastradero Road shows the Veterans Affairs Hospital at upper left, Gunn High School at the top, and the pharmaceutical company Syntex at the center.

PALO ALTO'S MAY FETE PARADE, C. 1950. The May Fete Parade has been held every first Saturday in May for over 85 years, becoming a long-running Palo Alto institution. (Courtesy Palo Alto Children's Theatre Archive, photograph by Anita Fowler.)

PALO ALTO CITY HALL, C. 1953. Pictured at the center of this image at the intersection of Embarcadero Road and Newell Road is the Palo Alto City Hall. The large vacant lot behind the building would later become the location of the main library.

CITY HALL AND DEVELOPMENT, 1954. The Palo Alto City Hall is seen here in the midst of mid-century development. From left to right, De Soto Drive, Walnut Street, Channing Avenue, and Stanley Way are all visible. The school at upper center is now called Duveneck Elementary School.

CITY HALL AND SWIMMING POOLS AT RINCONADA PARK, 1954. Palo Alto's old power plant and substation are at the right center of this photograph. The round pool actually served as a cooling station for the power plant and was later converted for swimming. Although the power plant has since been torn down, the pool and park are still operational. Embarcadero Road runs diagonally left to upper right.

PALO ALTO'S MAY FETE PARADE, C. 1954. The maypole can be seen in the image at left, behind the troop of Scouts saluting the flag. Above, a large float passes the Central Electric building. (Courtesy Palo Alto Children's Theatre Archive, photograph by Anita Fowler.)

PALO ALTO COURTHOUSE UNDER CONSTRUCTION, 1958. The courthouse on Grant Avenue is being built at the center of this photograph, while the Oregon Expressway underpass is at lower right. At Birch and California Streets is the old Safeway store that is now a tavern called Antonio's Nut House. J. J. and F. Grocery, at upper right, is located on College Avenue and El Camino Real.

CALIFORNIA AVENUE AND EL CAMINO REAL, 1960. The building at lower right with the pointed roof housed the Shirt-Tail Restaurant and is now occupied by the Olive Garden. The courthouse is prominent at the right. One can identify the old Palo Alto Firehouse on Park Boulevard, upper left, by its peaked roof and large double doors. Emergency vehicles were located in the building to its left.

COOLEY LANDING, 1950s. This area served as the dump for residents of San Mateo County. In those days, recycling was almost unheard of; everything from old tires to toxic paints was routinely bulldozed into the bay or burned. Some large bay-front developments are built on this kind of fill.

MIDDLEFIELD AND EMBARCADERO ROADS, 1951. The Walter Hayes School stands on this corner. The Palo Alto Junior Museum and Zoo at Rinconada Park is at lower right.

PALM DRIVE AND ARBORETUM, 1954. It is difficult to distinguish the arboretum, located in the eucalyptus grove at lower left. In the center is the open field where the Stanford Shopping Center would later be built. El Camino Real is at the right, along with El Palo Alto, the tall tree that is the living symbol of the city of Palo Alto. Also note Menlo Park and in the right corner, the old Dibble Army Hospital, which would soon become part of SRI.

SITE OF STANFORD SHOPPING CENTER, 1949. El Camino Real runs through the middle of this photograph. Palo Alto Hospital (now Hoover Pavilion) is the white building in the cluster of trees near the lower right corner. The big open area in the upper left is now the site of the Palo Alto Library and city hall.

STANFORD SHOPPING CENTER UNDER CONSTRUCTION. The newly grated site of the future Stanford Shopping Center is pictured at left in 1954. Hoover Pavilion is visible in the foreground. The upper tree line marks San Francisquito Creek, the border between San Mateo and Santa Clara Counties. Below, in 1957, more of the shopping center has been constructed, including the parking lot. Hoover Pavilion is at the left, and the new Sand Hill Road heads off to the right while El Camino passes along in the lower left corner.

STANFORD SHOPPING CENTER OPEN FOR BUSINESS.
The view above right was taken from above the
Stanford Golf Course, just behind the Buck Estate at
Alpine Road, looking east down Sandhill Road to the
new Stanford Shopping Center, finally operational. The
photograph below shows, from left to right, the old
Palo Alto water tower (far left), the Hoover Pavilion,
the Circle, El Camino Park, and San Francisquito
Creek running along the bottom. Some Menlo Park
houses stand on the other side of the creek. It appears
as though all of the cars on El Camino are stopped for
the light in front of the mall.

STANFORD SHOPPING CENTER, *c.* **1958.** The quickly filling parking lot surrounds the shopping complex, pictured shortly after its completion. San Francisquito Creek can be seen below the line of trees in the lower right.

TOWN AND COUNTRY VILLAGE, *C.* 1951. The Town and Country shopping center was captured from two angles while still under construction. The Greer family, large landowners in Palo Alto, had a home that once stood where the complex was eventually built. In the image above right, Stanford Stadium is at lower left and Alma Street and the railroad tracks at upper right. The characteristic long, low roofline of the shopping center is just taking shape at upper left, along El Camino Real. Below, a large gravel company is located between the Circle and Town and Country Village. Note that the railroad tracks spur off to allow train cars to enter and be filled with rocks or gravel.

TOWN AND COUNTRY VILLAGE, 1954. Here the shopping center is open for business across the street from Stanford Stadium and Palo Alto High School. The complex included a nice children's park with a merry-go-round and electric train. Alma Street and the railroad tracks can be seen in the lower part of the image.

PALO ALTO'S MAY FETE PARADE THROUGH THE YEARS. Shown here are more images of the long-running May Fete Parade in downtown Palo Alto. The photograph above was taken in 1958 and the one below in 1972. (Courtesy Palo Alto Children's Theatre Archive, photographs by Anita Fowler.)

PROGRESSIVE AIRPORT, 1948. This airport, technically in Mountain View and its building denoted with a checked roof, was situated at Middlefield and San Antonio Roads near an Eichler housing tract. Note the screened-in greenhouses and the dairy farm at lower left. The railroad tracks and Alma Street can be seen in the upper right. The site of the screened-in greenhouses remains today.

PALO ALTO AIRPORT, C. 1948. Constructed in 1940, this airport operated at the end of Embarcadero Road, next to the Palo Alto Golf Course, built a bit later. Also nearby was the Palo Alto Yacht Harbor, which no longer exists. In the 1940s and 1950s, this airport was Adrian Hatfield's first choice from which to run his aerial photography missions.

PALO ALTO AIRPORT. The above photograph, taken in 1952, shows the area east of Highway 101 off Embarcadero Road. The subdivision in the lower right includes Daphne, Aster, Jasmine, and Wisteria Ways. At center right are an Eichler development and the old Palo Alto Drive-In movie theater. The Palo Alto municipal golf course would be built, at center, in 1956. The original Palo Alto Airport, located at the intersection of Embarcadero and Page Mill Roads, produced the program at right in 1935. This page advertises the Palo Alto Airport Air Circus and Dedication on July 4 of that year. The Palo Alto Airport eventually moved to its new site off Embarcadero Road and remains there today. (Courtesy Palo Alto Library.)

A complete and competent crew, ready night and day with service for air travelers, private pilots and operators.

ASSOCIATED AIR SERVICES, LTD.

Managers
PALO ALTO AIRPORT
PALO ALTO SCHOOL OF AVIATION
Phone 8313

HILLER HELICOPTER DEMONSTRATION, LATE 1940S. Helicopter pioneer Stanley Hiller Jr. was in his late teens when he became one of the world's three principal developers of vertical flight. Hiller designed the world's first successful coaxial helicopter and copters for the military. He was also the source of many UFO sightings above Palo Alto in the early 1950s. His father, Stanley Hiller Sr., was an engineer and inventor who taught Stanley Jr. how to fly at age 10. Hiller's plant, pictured here, was situated on Willow Road, then considered part of Palo Alto and now part of east Menlo Park.

HILLER HELICOPTERS IN MENLO PARK, 1949. Stanley Hiller opened up shop on Willow Road in 1949; note the sign on the roof of the plant reading "Hiller-Copters of Palo Alto." Henry J. Kaiser provided funding in the early days of research. In the 1950s, during the Korean War, Hiller was producing the H-23 for the military. In 1966, during the Vietnam War, he lost a contract for helicopter production to Hughes Aircraft and subsequently closed Hiller-Copters.

EAST PALO ALTO, C. 1948. By the late 1940s, East Palo Alto developments were going strong. The image above captures the duck pond and yacht harbor in the distance, the airport, and the unfinished golf course in the center. Highway 101 runs in the lower right. The boat harbor, shown in the close-up view below, is no longer in existence. The Sea Scouts were headquartered at the Palo Alto Boat Harbor, and many private boat owners also enjoyed it over the years. When San Francisquito Creek was rerouted to gain more land for the golf course, however, the ecosystem of the harbor was drastically altered, and nearly constant dredging was required to keep it free of silt. Eventually, the costs of maintenance became too much for the city to bear, and the harbor was shut down.

CALIFORNIA AVENUE AT THE SOUTHERN PACIFIC RAILROAD, 1953. Pictured here are, from left to right, Holland Building Material, T-H Building Supply, Emmits Book Store, and in the lower right, the old fire station with a tower for sounding the alarm. Note the tower's shadow. Every Christmas, the firehouse put on a fantastic display, complete with an electric train that ran all around the building and through the palm trees.

PAGE MILL ROAD AT THE SOUTHERN PACIFIC RAILROAD, 1967. Page Mill Road dead-ends at the center of this photograph, while Oregon Expressway travels under Alma Street and the tracks. Note the railroad spur that lets train cars load and unload at the supply buildings. The tracks cut down to the lower right, heading to Los Altos, Los Gatos, and Santa Cruz. The bat wing–shaped building no longer exists.

MIDDLEFIELD AND SAN ANTONIO ROADS, 1952. Montrose Avenue and Southerland Drive are visible at the left. The commercial real estate firm of Perry and Ariaga owned much of the open land in early Palo Alto, Mountain View, and many other peninsula communities. The company, which recently built the new Stanford Stadium, has been the largest owner of commercial property in the Santa Clara Valley since the early 1950s. The former Progressive Airport and flight school can be seen at upper right.

FUTURE SITE OF NEW STANFORD INDUSTRIAL PARK, C. 1967. The swath of open space in the foreground provides a glimpse into Palo Alto's continued success after its postwar and technological boom; this would become the site of the continued development of the Stanford Industrial Park. Even more land had been set aside after the initial development of the complex, as it was quickly filled to capacity with electronics businesses. Ford Aerospace would become a tenant in the New Stanford Industrial Park, occupying a section along the loop road (pictured), called Fabian Way.

UNIVERSITY AVENUE CIRCLE, C. 1949. The above image provides an unusual perspective of the Circle, the University Avenue interchange. The train tracks run vertically through the center, accompanied by the station at lower right. The image below gives another view of the "gates to the city" in a long shot of University Avenue hosting a Christmas parade.

ALMA AVENUE AND EL CAMINO REAL. University Avenue Circle occupies the center of the image above, with Alma Avenue and El Camino Real running parallel through the center. The underpass was constructed to route the burgeoning car traffic up University Avenue without having to stop for the frequent commuter trains, which still travel alongside Alma Avenue. Below is an advertisement for one of the many businesses to establish itself "on the Circle" through the years: Smith's "On the Circle" Sporting Goods. Note the Davenport prefix.

EL CAMINO REAL NEAR SAN ANTONIO ROAD, 1970. Lozano's Car Wash, with its unmistakable pronged roofline, stands on the west side of El Camino Real; above that, also on the west side, is the Cabaña Hotel, which was built by Doris Day. Del Medio Avenue and Fayette Drive appear in the foreground.

OREGON EXPRESSWAY AND ALMA STREET, 1967. Page Mill Road and Park Boulevard run along the lower left of the image. In the 1950s, Fentron Industries was located in the longest, most narrow metal warehouse. The company sold aluminum doors and windows. Also note Colorado Street and the train heading north.

OPPOSITE: VIEW FROM EL CAMINO REAL AND PAGE MILL ROAD, 1953. This view, looking west to the foothills of the Coastal Range, shows the new Varian Associates building at lower left. Varian, a microwave technology pioneer, was the first tenant in the Stanford Industrial Park and reaped the obvious, if temporary, benefit of an increasingly rare view of California's open space.

THREE

COMMERCIAL DEVELOPMENT, LARGE AND SMALL

Radio research started locally as early as 1908 and evolved into a new industry—electronics. The early inventions of William Hewlett and David Packard and brothers Russell and Sigurd Varian started a new age of technology in Palo Alto. Both the Varian brothers and Hewlett and Packard were students at Stanford University and studied under Professors Terman and Hansen.

After World War II, Stanford University dedicated large areas of Stanford land for research and development in this new era of electronics and medical and space research. The designated land encompassed the Page Mill Road corridor by El Camino Real and College Terrace and traveled west to Junipero Serra Avenue.

The Stanford Industrial Park was then laid out and developed on the Page Mill Road–El Camino Real corridor. This age of electronics was not only happening in and around Palo Alto and Stanford; it was also going strong in San Carlos and Redwood City. Companies such as Litton Industries of San Carlos, Dalmo Victor of Belmont, and Itel McCullough of San Carlos were all up and running during the boom.

After initially opening in a garage at 367 Addison Avenue in 1938, Hewlett-Packard emerged in South Palo Alto in 1942. Bill Hewlett and David Packard were studying at Stanford University under the guidance of Frederick Terman, head of the School of Engineering. One of Hewlett-Packard's early developments was a tunable audio oscillator, which was used in sound production for the animated film *Fantasia* by Disney Studios. When World War II broke out, Bill Hewlett was called into the Army Signal Corps, and David Packard stayed on to run plant operations. Hewlett-Packard produced many devices to help win the war.

In 1942, Hewlett-Packard built a plant near Page Avenue and Alma Street, near the railroad tracks and Hueling Engineering. The firm's next plant was constructed at 1501 Page Mill Road in 1955. The author's mother, Margery Hatfield, worked for Hewlett-Packard at the Page Mill plant for 15 years. The company, which treated employees well, held great picnics at Little Basin, a private campground in the nearby Santa Cruz Mountains. Mike, the author's brother, attended Stanford as an engineering graduate student and, for his birthday, received one of Hewlett-Packard's first handheld calculators with a price tag of $295 in 1977.

The Varian brothers, Russell and Sigurd, started their research in a basement at the Stanford physics corner under the guidance of William W. Hansen. Radar (originally an acronym for "Radio Detection and Ranging") was invented in the early 1900s. But the Varians had an idea for perfecting radar through the development of a powerful microwave amplifier called a Klystron. A former airline pilot, Sigurd convinced his brother of the need to develop this technology, and to build it immediately for the war effort. Superior radar, based on the Klystron, helped in detecting bombers and fighter planes and aided in a turning point for the Allied victory during World War II. The Varian brothers began in San Carlos in 1948 and moved to Palo Alto Industrial Park in 1952, to be the first tenant of the new industrial park. Other items that Varian Associates developed were analytical instruments such as the spectrophotometer and the magnetometer.

New companies continued to spring up overnight, while established businesses like Varian and Hewlett-Packard grew by leaps and bounds. Lockheed Missiles and Space came into the Stanford Industrial Park in 1955, and starting in 1957, Sputnik hastened the pace for the military to create new weapons technology. Ballistic missiles and new satellite programs were started to keep ahead of the Russians. Lockheed also worked closely with other companies of the Stanford Complex on technical projects.

In 1964, Syntex moved to the Palo Alto complex. The company developed naproxyn, a non-steroidal anti-inflammatory drug, and also produced medical diagnostic instruments to detect drugs and alcohol. Alza spun off from Syntex and established its own corporation at the industrial park. Many of these new medical technologies were put into practice at the Veterans Hospital.

Stanford electrical engineer Dean Watkins and Richard Johnson, a microwave tube researcher at Hughes Aircraft, teamed up to form the defense and communications firm Watkins-Johnson. In 1957, Beckman Instruments began developing printed circuitry and semiconductors. Then, in 1959, several scientists that worked at Beckman Instruments split off on their own to form the Fairchild Semiconductor Corporation. Other newcomers to the Stanford Industrial Park were IBM and Xerox Reprographics, Eastman Kodak, the *Wall Street Journal*, and the Stanford Medical Center. The Xerox facility became the company's world-renowned Palo Alto Research Center, also known as Xerox PARC, the inventors of the computer mouse, graphical user interface, and other pioneering works. The first complete electronic circuit on a silicon chip was created by Robert Noyce, who with Gordon Moore founded Intel Corporation and brought his new company to the area.

During its first decade, the industrial corridor filled up, and the city fathers created two more areas for expansion—by 101, and San Antonio Road and Fabian Way. Philco Ford and Ford Aerospace came to the second industrial complex in 1958.

Although the great technology industry of today started in a garage (Hewlett-Packard) and in apricot drying sheds, other companies contracted large complexes of multiple buildings. Some of the early builders of the Stanford Industrial Park and other commercial sites in Palo Alto were Howard J. White, Goodenough General Contractors (a leader in Palo Alto until the late 1950s), E. A. Hathaway, Wheatly Construction, Barrett and Hilp (early school builders), Carl Holvic, and Vance Brown.

OPEN LAND, 1947. In this photograph, the area between College Terrace, California Avenue, and Page Mill Road reveals plenty of room for industrial expansion. Mayfield Elementary School is located at the bottom. Perhaps no one could have dreamed then what this land would be like today, but nonetheless the site was well planned out for the future. It went from dairy land to high-tech, all in a 10-year period from 1947 to 1957. Varian came in 1952, Lockheed in 1954, and Hewlett-Packard in 1955.

Bayshore's Finest

- **Hamburger Sandwich 25c**
  Made of freshly-ground western beef (we grind our own)

- **½ Fried Spring Chicken $1.00**
  On buttered toast, French-fries, vegetable, and salad

- Fresh Strawberry Sundae 30c
- Hot Fudge Sundae 35c
- Hot Butterscotch Sundae 35c

- **Chopped Sirloin Steak 85c**
  Made from freshly-ground western loin of beef with potatoes, vegetable, salad, roll and butter

- **Fried Fresh Jumbo Shrimp 85c**
  Served on buttered toast with French-fries, vegetable, and salad

- **Special Club Steak $1.10**
  With French-fries, vegetable, and salad

- Hot Caramel Sundae 35c
- Banana Split 40c
- Milk Shakes 25c

• Waffles and Coffee 35c

BREAKFAST ▬ LUNCH ▬ DINNER

GUSTIN DRIVE IN
BAYSHORE HIGHWAY • EAST PALO ALTO
Open 6 a.m.–1 a.m. Daily; Friday & Saturday 6 a.m.–3 a.m.
Two Blocks North of University

GUSTIN DRIVE-IN. Just a short drive up 101 from the Stanford Industrial Park lay East Palo Alto. This restaurant was situated on the Bayshore Highway (now Freeway), one of the main north-south thoroughfares on the peninsula. The advertisement, like many that appear in this book, features prices that indicate a time many years ago, likely mid-20th century, when half of a fried chicken might cost you $1 and a club steak just $1.10.

MATADERO CREEK, 1954. The creek can be distinguished as a curvy tree line snaking through the increasingly dense mix of homes and industry in Barron Park. Parts of this creek flow through what is now protected marshland and can be viewed while on the Baylands Trail Tour, an interpretive route along the Bay Trail, which runs around the entire San Francisco Bay. Hanover Street turns 90 degrees in the center of this image.

Kay's Beauty Salon . . .

Formerly The Personality Beauty Salon

ALL TYPES
OF
PERMANENT
WAVING

EVENINGS BY
APPOINTMENT

*Soft Water
Used in
All Operations*

Telephone

Palo Alto 6264

359 UNIVERSITY AVE.

featuring
TINTING
SCALP TREATMENTS
EXPERT MANICURIST

Walk Through the Flower Shop to Our Mezzanine Salon

Cardinal

BEAUTY PARLOR

The
" WAY TO CHARM"

- PERMANENT WAVING
- TINTING & BLEACHING
- HAIR SHAPING
- SCALP TREATMENTS
  for
MEN AND WOMEN
★ INDIVIDUAL BOOTHS

MR. KLEIN   MR GILBERT

Phone
PALO ALTO 3823

540 RAMONA

BEAUTY SUPPLY ADVERTISEMENTS. These advertisements, taken from the local phone directory, both promote area beauty parlors. Today fewer beauty parlors remain, replaced by many downtown salons and day spas.

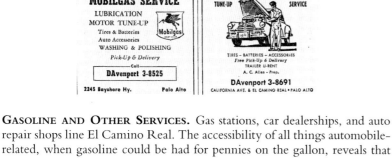

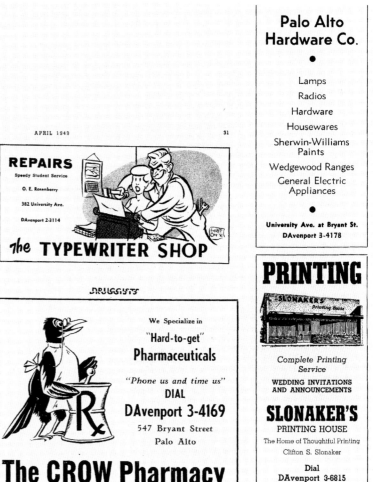

GASOLINE AND OTHER SERVICES. Gas stations, car dealerships, and auto repair shops line El Camino Real. The accessibility of all things automobile-related, when gasoline could be had for pennies on the gallon, reveals that mobility was of the utmost importance to Americans. These advertisements announce the various gas stations, as well as the assortment of other services and goods, available to the citizens of mid-1900s Palo Alto.

VARIAN ELECTRONICS, 1954. Varian stands at Hansen Way and El Camino Real. Note the hotel with a swimming pool in the lower portion of the image and the Chimalus Avenue cul-de-sac above. The literal and figurative overlap of home and commercial high-tech industries through the years was just par for the course in Palo Alto.

EL CAMINO REAL, C. 1955. Leland and Stanford cross Birch and Ash Streets in this tucked-away little neighborhood on the right. In the center, one can see the vast expanse of land occupied by the Stanford Industrial Park, with Varian on the left and the under-construction Hewlett-Packard on the right. Running north to south is El Camino Real, on the right, and Alma Avenue, running parallel on the left. The College Terrace neighborhood juts out in the right center.

WHERE PALO ALTO WENT, AFTER WORK. A popular tradition among those working at the Stanford Industrial Park was to carpool in a different employee's car each day, taking turns to be the driver to and from the restaurants. Many of these restaurants were extremely popular with residents of Palo Alto, particularly Andre's L'Omelette and Chez Yvonne. Andre's L'Omelette, more commonly referred to as "L'Ommies," was known as a Friday restaurant, because its fine bar and live music attracted working folk by mid-afternoon Friday and prevented them from returning to the job again until Monday.

PAGE MILL ROAD, 1955. This view of Page Mill looks east over southern Palo Alto. Open land covers the near (west) side of El Camino, and not too much is on the other side. Hewlett-Packard will soon occupy the large building in the foreground, still under construction here.

LOCKHEED MISSILES, 1955. In the foreground are what appear to be the few small structures of a farmstead. Directly adjacent, the freshly leveled ground will become Lockheed Missiles on Page Mill Road.

"Where Device and Care Prolong Wear"

J. B. BLOIS, Proprietor

STANFORD LAUNDRY CO.

252 Forest Avenue   Phone 6108

LAUNDRY AND CLEANING ADVERTISEMENTS. Along with the boom of industrial and technological commerce in Palo Alto came a service industry to accommodate the influx of new workers and residents. These two advertisements promote laundering services in downtown Palo Alto. The Stanford Laundry Company (above) was featured in the Palo Alto High School yearbook.

CARDINAL CLEANERS

DRIVE IN SERVICE

A Faster, Finer Cleaning Service

HOME OWNED

PICK-UP AND DELIVERY SERVICE

Bundle Drop For After Hours

HATS CLEANED AND BLOCKED

4-HOUR SPECIAL SERVICE

Phone DAvenport 3-9240

625 Ramona Street   Palo Alto

PAGE MILL ROAD AND FOOTHILL EXPRESSWAY. 1955. The new Hewlett-Packard building is visible in the distance. College Terrace appears in the upper left corner. In the foreground, new roads have been paved and walls erected as yet another new tenant is established at the Stanford Industrial Park.

JUNIPERO SERRA AND PAGE MILL ROADS, 1955. The large building at the center of this view is Stanford's Ryan High Energy Lab, now demolished. The flat square nearby is a reservoir that remains today. This area, with the roads intersecting at lower left, is now completely covered by homes on the Stanford Campus. College Terrace is seen in the upper right, with Stanford University in the background.

MODELED BY BARBARA DUNBAR

Larry's
FLOWER SHOP

340 UNIVERSITY AVENUE   PALO ALTO

MODELED BY MARGARET INGALLS AND MEREDY MANNING

Joseph Magnin's

MODELED BY MARILYN MARTIN AND AUDREY HURLEY

FINEST STYLING AND QUALITY IN
CASUAL AND ACTIVE SPORTSWEAR

Phelps-Terkel

MODELED BY BOB SMITH AND PAT HOFFACKER

Gleim's

OVER 100 STERLING SILVER
PATTERNS TO CHOOSE FROM

YEARBOOK ADVERTISEMENTS, C. 1951. Among the clothiers advertised here are Joseph Magnin's, Phelps-Terkel, and Gleim's, obviously all quite popular with Palo Alto's youth.

**HEWLETT-PACKARD
BUILDINGS ON PAGE
MILL ROAD, 1956.**
Barron Park is visible
in the distance. All the
parking lots seem to be
full, indicating business
was good.

OPEN LAND, C. 1957. Page Mill Road heads straight out to Junipero Serra in the far distance. The S-shaped railroad on the left operated before and after Oregon Avenue and Page Mill Road were connected by the underpass at Alma Street. El Camino Real and Page Mill meet at the center of the photograph.

BOOKS AND BREAD. This page from an undated directory features advertisements for the Alcove bookstore on Ramona and for Palo Alto Bread, once located on Homer Avenue.

STANFORD INDUSTRIAL PARK, 1958. The area is pictured in the midst of its great transformation from farmland to industrial park. At lower right are Oregon Expressway and Colorado Avenue as they meet Alma Street. College Terrace is in the distant center and Hoover Tower at upper right.

MODELED BY BETTY REDDING AND JIM TIDDY

THE CAMERA SHOP

541 BRYANT STREET

Congratulates Paly High's '51 Grads And Wishes Them Godspeed

MODELED BY MIKE ARNSTEIN

John C. Skrabo's
FLOWERS FOR EVERYBODY

490 UNIVERSITY AVENUE   DA 2-2813

MODELED BY JANE ROODHOUSE AND MERLE FLATTLEY

Come In and See Our Wide
Selection of Print Shirts

Schneider's
ROBERT JORDAN STORE FOR MEN
330 UNIVERSITY AVENUE   DA 3-9342

MODELED BY ELISSA WANK AND CAROLL ZSCHOKKE

Hit Dad for a Portable

DeFrees OFFICE EQUIPMENT

463 UNIVERSITY AVENUE   DA 3-4129

YEARBOOK ADVERTISEMENTS, 1951. These promotions feature a variety of goods catering to college-bound seniors, including a portable typewriter, menswear, and even cameras.

PAGE MILL ROAD AND OREGON AVENUE, C. 1958. Page Mill Road connects to Oregon Expressway and Alma Street via the underpass. Junipero Serra Road (now Foothill Expressway) runs parallel to Alma in the distance. Varian, Hewlett-Packard, and Lockheed Missiles, among others, will soon cover all this open land up to Foothill Expressway.

JUNIPERO SERRA AND PAGE MILL ROADS, 1961. At the intersection of Junipero Serra and Page Mill, open space gives way to burgeoning industry and suburban tract housing. The area in the upper right corner, Coyote Hill, served as an army camp during World War II.

Don Kenyon shows Ann Haile and Lane Spencer a bottle of perfume from Kenyon's wide selection.

Kenyon's
PRESCRIPTION PHARMACY
425 University Avenue
Phone DAvenport 3-5181   PALO ALTO, CALIF.
HOUSE OF BETTER COSMETICS
AND PERFUMES

the skylight

for artists' materials   •   444 cowper   palo alto

Paula Kursh, Virginia Biondi, and Towru Ikeda inspect the newest and best in art supplies at the Skylight.

YEARBOOK ADVERTISEMENTS, 1954. The famous and still-thriving Peninsula Creamery is featured in the lower left corner of this advertisement space. As it was then, the creamery remains an extremely popular hangout for residents and college students alike.

PALY'S FAVORITE FOUNTAIN
For over 25 years

Pam Marley, Jim Hubbard, Jean Christy, and Bob Haight stop in at the Penn for one of those famous milkshakes.

Peninsula Creamery

No doubt about it. Al Brenner and Ann Cromwell go for this colorful sportshirt at Christy's.

BE IT A SPORTSHIRT — CORDS — DENIMS — OR
"WHAT HAVE YOU" — CHRISTY'S HAS IT

T. C. CHRISTY CO.
F. V. COCHRAN
170 UNIVERSITY AVE.   DAVENPORT 3-5321

OPPOSITE: PALO ALTO MOVES SOUTH. This view was taken from above Highway 101. Eichler housing tracts can be seen in a circular pattern, both at the center, adjacent to the Palo Alto Drive-In, and in the distance on the right. The open expanses of land beyond the new development in the foreground speak to the burgeoning development of South Palo Alto around 1952.

BUILDING OUR NEIGHBORHOODS

The year is 1953, the month March, and the orchards are in full bloom. It is early morning, windy and very cold, but an extremely clear day—perfect conditions for a photographic mission. My father and I are bundled up in leather, fleece-lined flight jackets. The door is open in the Cessna plane, and we have strapped ourselves and our equipment in safely, cameras at the ready. The aroma of apricot blossoms is rich and sweet. The colors of the mustard grass, the orchards, and nurseries are intense—greens, yellows, reds, and white,

something like looking down on a very large quilt that has bright squares and rectangles embroidered on it. Black-and-white photography cannot capture those brilliant colors, but it is still deeply imprinted on my mind to this day.

Joseph Eichler has purchased the ranch lands and nurseries near the Alma and Charleston Road areas. He has just started the tract by Charleston Road at Alma and is in the grading stage. Heavy equipment is everywhere, and men are working at the site. Other

builders have also bought up land because the building boom is on.

We are flying at about 1,000 feet when my father shouts out, "Find some new circles scratched out of the roadway." I cannot hear well with the door off and the engine noise drowning out any conversation. We circle the area and I spot it. "Circles . . . three of them at 3:00!" There are three distinct circles, one large and two smaller ones that connect with the big one. As soon as we spot the target, the pilot starts circling above

it. I hand my father the large Fairchild F-56 wide-angle lens, and he starts shooting a series of photographs right over the site and from all angles and directions. I reload the aerial cameras with spare film packs as fast as my father can shoot. We make passes and document other areas along Alma Street, where many other tracts are being built by different contractors and developers.

The focus of this book is post–World War II, when the demand for housing and education surged. The population of Palo Alto in the 1940s was about 17,000. By the 1950s, the population had hit 25,000, and by 1953, more than 34,000. A huge housing shortage developed because Palo Alto had already been built out to its city limits. People were sharing homes and garages and living in sheds. During this era, 5 to 10 families were moving here every day. Attractive loan packages offered to veterans made it easy for them to buy new homes—if they could find any.

Builders and developers, noting the shortage by 1948, went to work. Sterns and Price and Barret and Hilp built the Boulware Tract between Newhall and Channing Roads. Many other developers followed suit. One of the earliest new developments by Joseph Eichler was the Barron Park Bol Tract. The homes constructed there were primarily of a modern design with low-pitched roofs and glass clerestory windows—the unique style created by Eichler. These new developments sat primarily south of the city limits, so new construction pushed the city in that direction, toward Oregon Avenue and all the way to Highway 101 at Bayshore Road.

Joseph Eichler started buying farmland, nurseries, and ranches in 1948 and, in 1949 and 1950, purchased most of the land he later developed. According to the unpublished book *Palo Alto Moves South* by Adrian R. Hatfield, by 1951 Eichler wanted every family to enjoy the American Dream of home ownership for a price tag of only $10,000 to $14,000, with monthly payments of $55 to $60 and no down payment. The idea was to buy the land cheap, develop and build at the best price, and turn out an outstanding family home for all.

Eichler's architect, Robert Anshen, created a new style of building, what he called the modern contemporary style. He worked with small lots, fast construction times, slab floors, single-wall construction (no sheetrock, as paneling was attached directly to the frame), and cheap, efficient radiant heating through coiled hot water pipes weaving throughout the slab floor. That idea goes back some 2,000 years to the Roman palace builders who used heated water in clay pipes in the floors. On the exterior of the homes, Anshen used T-111 plywood siding. Tall, open window walls and near-flat roofs were also incorporated into his design. Beamed ceilings created an open feeling. Atrium gardens in the entryway were a trademark, as were open courtyards. Fireplaces, cabinets, appliances, tile, and carpets were all included in the package—no extras.

Eichler also had his own style of planning and building the subdivisions. His circular or organic shapes became innovative street designs. In Eichler's firm, Nolte Engineering, John Hogan served as vice president and managed all engineering layout, street mapping, and grading. Eichler's first subdivision was the Barron Park Bol Tract (1949); followed by Park Boulevard, by Charleston Road and Alma Street (1951); Green Gables (1951); Fairmeadow, off Alma between East Meadow Drive and Charleston Road (1952); and Royal Manor (1957). Other Eichler developments showed up in San Mateo, Daly City, Redwood City, Sunnyvale, Santa Clara, and one of his last across the bay in Walnut Creek. Adrian Hatfield shot aerial photographs for Eichler; in addition, he helped create some of the large murals showing the parcels and streets in the subdivision, key shopping areas, and restaurants. When someone pushed a button for shopping or a hospital, that location would light up on the map. Eichler homes that sold in 1950 for $10,000 are now worth $900,000 in Palo Alto.

Other new subdivisions sprang up and spread out southeast to Colorado Road, Crescent Avenue, St. Louis and Ross Roads, and Greer and Middlefield Roads. Some 30 new subdivisions for single-family homes were built from 1947 to 1960.

With the dwindling availability of land and housing in the Palo Alto area, apartment complexes became the next big push. Apartment builder and large landowner S. T. Tan of China was one of the pioneer developers of apartments in Palo Alto in 1960. Then the 1970s brought the emergence of townhouses and apartment conversions to individually owned condominiums. After the condominium boom, land prices reached an all-time high. Homeowners wanted maximum square footage and maximum lot coverage. This was the start of monster homes in Palo Alto. Many single-family homes were razed to build new, bigger ones.

Palo Alto has been one of the most sought-after residential areas on the peninsula from its inception, through the electronics boom to today. It remains one of the most desirable choices for education, employment, and a home site—if you can afford it!

BARRON PARK, 1947. Barron Park is a nice neighborhood lying west of El Camino Real and south of Page Mill Road in South Palo Alto. Seen here are Josina, Kendall, Barron, and La Donna Streets, with Matadero Creek at the left along the tree line.

BARRON PARK, C. 1947. These Barron Park buildings were part of one of the first sections of Joseph Eichler's development, called the Bol Tract. The B&C Cabinet Shop supplied the cabinets and millwork for Eichler's tracts.

CHARLESTON AND ALMA STREETS, 1949. Heavy machinery grates the land for the first Eichler developments. These circular streets were a new concept widely accepted at the time. Today Eichlers are controversial; some love them and some do not. Moffett Naval Air Station, seen at upper right, housed weather balloons, blimps, and dirigibles before and during World War II.

INSIDE HANGAR NO. 1 AT MOFFETT FIELD, C. 1931. A fleet of navy planes rests inside Moffett Field's Hangar No. 1, visible in the upper right of the previous image. (Courtesy U.S. Navy.)

WILBUR JUNIOR HIGH SCHOOL, JUNE 1949. In this view, Meadow Street is at the left, along with Herbert Hoover School on Charleston Road. Mitchell Park lies in the center. A large Eichler development can be seen below, identified by its circular layout and the homes' characteristic low A-frame rooflines.

CEMENT FOR NEW DEVELOPMENT. Many trades and services developed out of the booming construction business in Palo Alto in the mid-1900s. These advertisements promote several cement companies around Mountain View and Palo Alto.

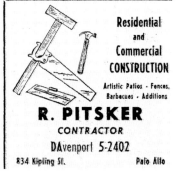

BAYSHORE HIGHWAY AND AMARILLO STREET, 1953. Here a circle of Eichlers splits off of Greer Street. This photograph would be difficult to shoot today because the trees have grown higher than the houses. The Palo Alto drive-in theater is just off Highway 101.

MERNER LUMBER COMPANY, 1947. Merner Lumber supplied wood and materials to many of the early builders. The firm later became Hubbard and Johnson Lumber, operating from the same location. The future site of the Town and Country Village shopping center is just across the road on the right side of the image, where it appears there may be a carnival going on.

MERNER LUMBER AND HARDWARE ADVERTISEMENT, C. 1949. These two advertisements for Merner demonstrate the wide variety of products and services available to builders and residents in the booming community. Merner sold its business to Hubbard and Johnson, which opened its doors about 1960. The mascot's nickname was "Mernie."

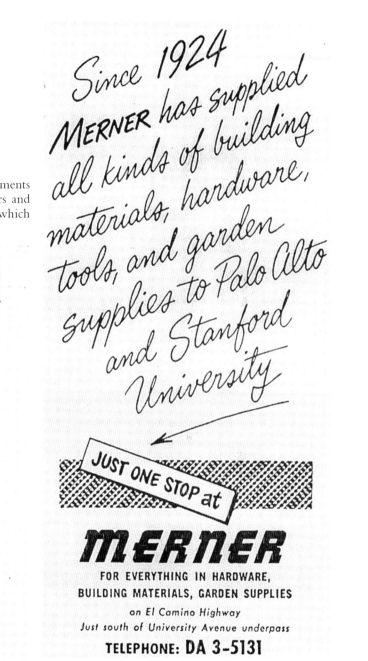

LUMBER
REDWOOD – PINE – FIR

"Kiln Dried Lumber a Specialty"

- ROOFING
- SHINGLES
- MILLWORK
- SASH & DOORS
- PLYWOOD
- HARDWARE

- INSULATION
- WALLBOARD
- TILEBOARD
- SHEET ROCK
- MASONITE
- PAINTS

- SAND & CEMENT
- WOOD PRESERVATIVES

- FENCE MATERIALS
- LATHING MATERIALS

"Mernie"

Phone DAvenport 3-5131

MERNER
LUMBER – HARDWARE

795 EL CAMINO REAL   **PALO ALTO**

Since 1924 MERNER has supplied all kinds of building materials, hardware, tools, and garden supplies to Palo Alto and Stanford University

JUST ONE STOP at

MERNER
FOR EVERYTHING IN HARDWARE, BUILDING MATERIALS, GARDEN SUPPLIES

on El Camino Highway
Just south of University Avenue underpass

TELEPHONE: DA 3-5131

EICHLER DEVELOPMENT, C. 1955. An Eichler development occupies the foreground, while the tall screen and fan-shaped grated earth of the Palo Alto Drive-In are visible in the background. Greer and Amarillo Streets and Bayshore Highway are located near the theater.

Meadow Park

Palo Alto's Greatest Home Value!

Compare square footage, features, planning, lot size and location, and you'll make the pleasant discovery that there just isn't another home value like Meadow Park. Here is genuine luxury for the discriminating homebuyer, value priced from $15,650 to $16,950!

3 bedrooms, 2 luxury baths plus complete Westinghouse built-in kitchen!

- Range, oven, dishwasher & disposall!
- Ash cabinets and paneling!
- Forced air perimeter heating.
- Two car garage with extra utility space!

plus many more fine home features!

$325 Down to Veterans
Excellent FHA terms, also

2 model homes furnished by PARK'S, of Palo Alto

To get to Meadow Park:
Drive south on Bayshore or El Camino to Embarcadero Rd. in Palo Alto. Turn right off Bayshore (left off El Camino) to Middlefield Rd. Turn south on Middlefield approximately 2 miles to Meadow Park. Model home phone: DA 4-2452.

a planned community by **brown & kauffmann**

Page 2—June 30, 1956   PENINSULA LIVING

MEADOW PARK DEVELOPMENT. The Brown and Kauffmann development company announces its planned community in Palo Alto. Note the fine print: homes were available to veterans with just a $325 down payment.

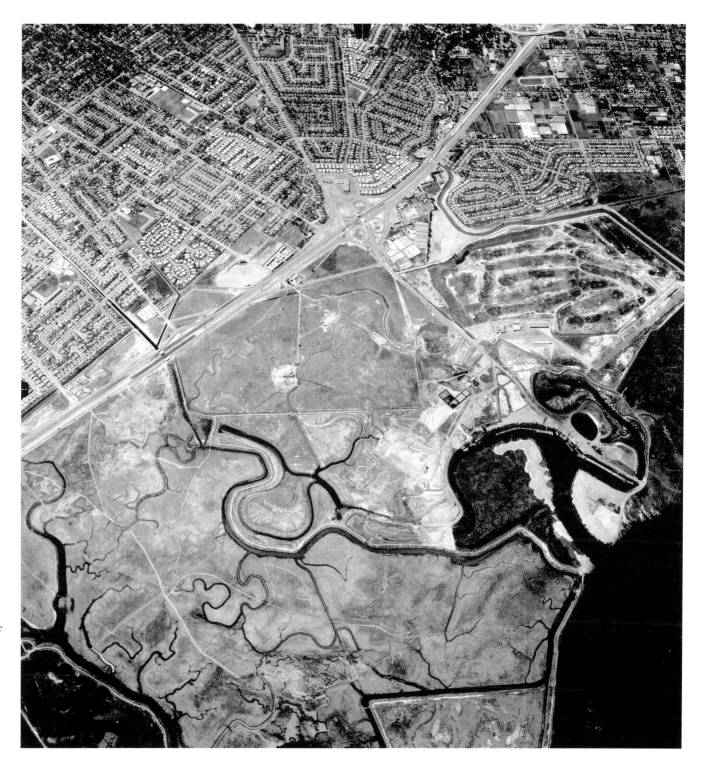

NEW DEVELOPMENTS TAKE OVER, C. 1956. Pictured here are the airport, golf course, duck pond, yacht harbor, and drive-in theater near the Eichler circular development in the upper left. The movie site is now home to Greer Park, and the waterway snaking down from 101 is Mayfield Slough. Highway 101 and Embarcadero are at upper center.

EICHLER'S ART, C. 1956. Only birds and people in airplanes got to enjoy this view of the circles, angles, curves, and cul-de-sacs of mid-20th-century Palo Alto.

WEST COAST GLASS. Some of the companies that found a firm foothold during Palo Alto's initial construction boom still prosper today, such as West Coast Glass, whose 1950 advertisement is featured here.

ARASTRADERO ROAD AT EL CAMINO REAL, 1958. Los Palos Avenue, Suzanne Drive, and McKellar Street all run off Arastradero Road. El Camino Way and East Meadow are at the left. The ubiquitous patterns of Eichler's planned community appear in the distance.

THE STANFORD ELECTRIC WORKS. Located at 304 High Street, this establishment still does business at the same location today.

DAHL PLUMBING. Once owned by Barry Anderson's brother Billy, Dahl Plumbing was one of the primary plumbing contractors in Palo Alto for homes and businesses. The company used Stanford's Hoover Tower as its insignia.

RICKEY'S RESTAURANT, 1947. The above view shows Rickey's Restaurant before the hotel was built on the site. At the time, both the eatery and the adjacent Elks Lodge were surrounded by orchards. The advertisement at right features both Rickey's locations: San Francisco and Palo Alto.

121

RICKEY'S RESTAURANT AND HOTEL, C. 1952. Seen under construction on El Camino Real and Arastradero Road, the Rickey's Restaurant and Hotel complex was a local landmark, at its height of popularity in the 1950s and 1960s. Construction extended back into the orchard at the upper part of the image. Just as the great old tank house at left was torn down for the expansion, Rickey's was razed in 2005–2006 to make way for houses and condominiums.

"Burrpp!"

Luncheon—all you can eat—95c

Dinner—all you can eat—$1.95

DINAH'S SHACK. This spot on El Camino Real is now the site of Trader Vic's Restaurant, but the landmark tower remains today. The swimming pool across the street was associated with the restaurant, along with the mobile-home park. The advertisements below feature both a pictorial view of the tower and a lighthearted take on the restaurant's satisfied customers.

L'Omelette's French Restaurant. Located on El Camino and Maybell, L'Omelette's was a popular eating, drinking, and dancing establishment. Palo Alto residents spent many pleasant hours hanging around the piano bar and fireplace. In the 1947 photograph at left, L'Ommie's is the larger structure and Clark's Charcoal Burgers the smaller. The undated advertisement below pays homage to the many names patrons gave the restaurant.

ARASTRADERO ROAD, C. 1948. Here Arastradero Road runs through Palo Alto's plentiful rows of apricots, pears, apples, and walnuts trees. Monroe Street is in the upper left, along with El Camino. Adobe Creek and Los Altos Avenue wind along the upper right, while Alta Mesa Cemetery lies to the lower right.

HOMER STREET AT EL CAMINO REAL, 1947. Merner Lumber, Hubbard and Johnson, and a number of other lumberyards occupied this location over the years. It currently houses the Palo Alto Medical Clinic. A traveling circus appears to be set up on the Greer home property, now the site of Town and Country Village.

MCELROY LUMBER COMPANY, C. 1947. McElroy Lumber Company was located on El Camino Way near the Old Barrel and El Camino Real. Supplying lumber for the new expansion of South Palo Alto, it was also one of the largest sources of materials for the influx of builders to the city.

185 MARTIN AVENUE. George E. Hogan, one of Palo Alto's early builders, constructed his home in 1942.

GEORGE HOGAN. Above, the Hogan brothers lean on their car, parked in front of their home on Hamilton. Below is the contractor's license for the construction of the Martin Avenue house. At that time, contractors were granted licenses for individual homes.

REGISTRATION CERTIFICATE

This is to certify that in accordance with the
Selective Service Proclamation of the President of the United States

George   Elmer   Hogan
(First name)   (Middle name)   (Last name)

185 Martin Ave Palo Alto California
(Place of residence)
(This will be identical with line 2 of the Registration Card)

has been duly registered this 26 day of April, 1942

C. Louise Graham
(Signature of registrar)

Registrar for Local Board 112 Palo Alto Calif.
(Number) (City or county) (State)

**THE LAW REQUIRES YOU TO HAVE THIS CARD IN YOUR
PERSONAL POSSESSION AT ALL TIMES**

D. S. S. Form 2
(Revised 6/9/41)   16—21631

(Registrant must sign here)

ARASTRADERO AND POMONA AVENUES, 1948. Orchards of pears, apricots, apples, and walnuts abounded throughout the entire Santa Clara Valley, and Palo Alto was no exception. In addition to the orchards, the city produced various types of fruits and flowers.

EARLY SOUTH PALO ALTO SUBDIVISION, 1949. Here the orchards whose trees once outnumbered homes in Palo Alto are becoming interspersed with the tract homes that now make up the bulk of the settlement. The post–World War II building boom witnessed the end of most farmsteads.

MIDDLEFIELD ROAD, 1949. Middlefield Road runs left to right, intersected by Charleston Road, running top to bottom before cutting right to meet San Antonio Road. Note the screened-in greenhouses and plowed fields with the farmhouse in the middle. Joseph Eichler and other builders purchased this open land in 1949 and 1950 at the beginning of the building boom.

MIDDLEFIELD AND CHARLESTON ROADS, 1949. Middlefield Road runs from the lower right corner and intersects with east Charleston in the center. The Eichler development at the far right is just getting started, as indicated by the circular grating pattern in the soil. It will include, among other streets, Redwood and Roosevelt Circle.

New Development, 1949. Both of these images depict burgeoning development along Alma Street, dotted with trees and running at the upper edge. Below left, workers have just begun to grade the surface for a new circular Eichler development.

EARLY BRENTWOOD SUBDIVISION, 1950. This view shows East Palo Alto at Pulgas Avenue and Highway 101. O'Connor Street and Pulgas Avenue intersect at the center left of the image, and the Palo Alto Airport can be seen in the upper left corner. Houses and greenhouses stand facing each other in the foreground as old agriculture meets new suburban settlement.

STERNS–PRICE DEVELOPMENT, 1951. Loma Verde Avenue and Waverly Street are at upper center, while East Meadow Drive and Emerson Streets are at lower center in this image. The Southern Pacific Railroad tracks run parallel to Alma Street at lower left.

PAINT CONTRACTORS. Among the many services to prosper with the construction boom in Palo Alto were, of course, house painters. At this time, one could get a house painted for the low price of just $385 and pay it off in increments of $12.62 per month.

SPRINGTIME IN GRAYSCALE, 1951. Highway 101 is visible in the distance of this San Antonio Road view. When flying over neighborhoods like this in February and March, the earth is a patchwork of fantastic greens, yellows, and pinks from all the flowers, trees, and fields in bloom. Alvin and Victory Streets are at right, and Mackay and San Antonio Avenue are at lower center.

EAST PALO ALTO, *C.* **1952.** Shown here are Willow Road and Bayshore Highway in East Palo Alto. Note the train tracks at left, curving out to the railroad bridge that crosses the marshes and bay. The buildings at lower right comprise the Veterans Hospital. Cooley Landing extends into the bay in the distance.

DISAPPEARING ORCHARDS, 1953. Arastradero Road cuts west through the soon-to-disappear orchards and plowed fields of this rich, fertile area. El Camino Real runs across the top. Some of the streets visible in these early developments are Georgia Avenue and Hubbart, Willmar, and Donald Drives.

PAGE MILL ROAD AND ALMA STREET, C. 1954. The empty plot of land at right is now the location of the Palo Alto Courthouse, and the park in the lower portion still exists. The photograph above appears to have been taken in the middle of a workday, as all the parking lots are full. Note the California Avenue train station at lower right, surrounded by vehicles. T&H Building Supply is the long, large building adjacent to the station; the company's advertisement is pictured at left.

STERNS–PRICE DEVELOPMENT, 1951. Ramona Street, Bryant Street, South Court, and Waverly Street run between El Verano and East Meadow Drive. The field in the foreground is the site of the large circular Eichler tract. Alma Street and the Caltrain tracks are at upper left.

EL CAMINO WAY AND EL CAMINO REAL, *C.* 1949. In this view, West Meadow Drive enters El Camino Way at the upper right. In the center are a used car lot and a dog kennel. El Camino Real spans just one lane in each direction with a passing lane in the center—a far cry from today's busy four-to-six-lane thoroughfare.

ALPINE INN. Formerly Rosottie's, the Alpine Inn was a stage stop along Alpine Road in the town of Portola Valley. In the 1870s, it served as a water stop for stagecoaches and logging teams, and through the years, it has also been a general store and an eatery. Today the Alpine Inn Beer Garden is a well-known place for families to visit and for post-game Stanford students to get a burger and a brew. Over the years, many students have flocked to "Zotts," as it is known by regulars, including John Kennedy. His name is carved in one of the large wooden picnic tables—a custom that has continued for years. The restaurant has been a popular hangout for electronic startup companies, from the very early days of electronics to the present dot-com magnates. It is also where most of this book was put together, after long hours researching at the Palo Alto Library.

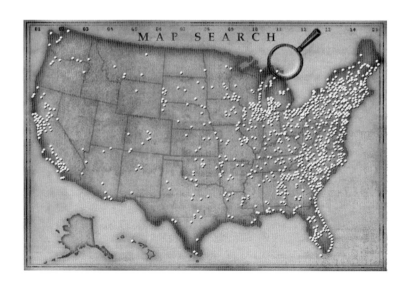